Vanished in the
Unknown Shade

VANISHED

in the

UNKNOWN SHADE

Poet Sidney Lanier's Montgomery Years

HELEN F. BLACKSHEAR

FOREWORD BY DOT MOORE

NewSouth Books
Montgomery

NewSouth Books
105 S. Court Street
Montgomery, AL 36104

Library of Congress Cataloging-in-Publication Data

ISBN 978-1-60306-261-9

Design by Randall Williams

Printed in the United States of America

To the Students,
Then, Now, and Future,
of Sidney Lanier High School

Night and Day

The innocent, sweet Day is dead.
Dark Night hath slain her in her bed.
O, Moors are as fierce to kill as to wed!
—Put out the light, said he.

A sweeter light than ever rayed
From star of heaven or eye of maid
Has vanished in the unknown Shade.
—She's dead, she's dead, said he.

Now, in a wild, sad after-mood
The tawny Night sits still to brood
Upon the dawn-time when he wooed.
—I would she lived, said he.

Star-memories of happier times,
Of loving deeds and lovers' rhymes,
Throng forth in silvery pantomimes.
—Come back, O Day! said he.

SIDNEY LANIER
Montgomery, Alabama, 1866

CONTENTS

FOREWORD

Helen Adele Friedman Blackshear

DOT MOORE

I met Helen on my first day as a teacher at Sidney Lanier High School, named for the subject of this book. My encounter with her enriched my life from that day in September 1954 until now, as she is a very pleasant memory.

Our first appointment was to attend the introductory faculty meeting. After brief introductions of the teachers, I was soon recoiling in horror from the principal who insulted one of the older teachers who stated, in a very gentle manner, that he could not see the scrawling on the blackboard. "Get up and move," he ordered. Ordered.

Next, the principal announced several strict rules that we teachers were to follow obediently. Then, the principal assigned each of us to an upcoming Friday football game where we were to sell popcorn and take up tickets! Aloud, I objected, stating those chores were not part of our duties as teachers. I was not aware that one did not speak out at *his* faculty meetings at Sidney Lanier High School. (Later, I was secretly acclaimed by a few of the faculty members after parents began assuming the football game tasks. Turned out the parents relished the football assignments!)

At the faculty meeting where I spoke out, Helen gently nudged me and shook her head "no." Standing near one another in the hall after the fated faculty meeting, Helen invited me to her house on Court Street, just across from the school. There, she told me that she, too, was a new teacher. She comforted me with the assurance that my words were not misguided, but this particular principal was not to be criticized. Never. She dared to help me in this unfamiliar role. She was always helpful to me and to others. She *never* turned down anyone who needed help.

This astute warning was my first gift from Helen. Her second gift was also at her house that same afternoon, where she presented me with a kitty, which I loved for years. I named the kitty Calpurnia—for Caesar's sterile wife, because I wanted no more kitties. But Helen knew the kitty was a male! Helen had a marvelous, warm chuckling laugh, and with great delight, she often told on me for my kitty-naming.

Her third gift to me was her willingness to assume my responsibility to complete a monthly attendance report, called "The Statistical Register." The monthly attendance report was based on the homeroom's morning roll calls. It was simple, unless the homeroom teacher enrolled a new student or a student left! After my performance at the first faculty meeting, I dared not make another mistake with the principal's office by submitting an erroneous attendance report. Helen quickly assessed my lack of math skills. We made a pact: I would keep the inventory of her classroom library (I could count books), and she would complete my complex monthly reports (as the students in my homeroom often came and went).

We both successfully finished that school year and never taught at Sidney Lanier High School again. She went on to Lee High School as an English teacher, and I went on to becoming a mother of four children. But our warm relationship continued.

There were many other gifts to follow: she sponsored me as a member of the Montgomery Press and Authors' Club and introduced me to well-known writers when we roomed together at the Alabama Writers' Conclave meetings at the University of Montevallo in the summers. Once, she graced my house as I invited my friends to hear her read poetry. My friends, in turn, bought all the books she had with her that afternoon.

Many years later, she told me that she was moving back to Tuscaloosa to a small cabin in the woods. To die, I assumed. I was right.

To know Helen, it is easier to state what she was not. She was never arrogant, never rude, never bragged, never highfalutin, never pretentious.

Helen could have claimed a high position in our socially conscious Montgomery community. She was the granddaughter of Bernard Friedman, a Hungarian immigrant who came to Tuscaloosa, Alabama, and made a fortune in the merchandising business. Helen was born Adele, named in part for her Hungarian-born grandmother, Adele. The Friedman Mansion in Tuscaloosa later became a museum when given to the University of Alabama by Helen's uncle, Hugo Friedman.

Helen was a graduate of Agnes Scott College, the South's preeminent and most expensive woman's college. She married into the Montgomery Blackshear family whose home is still one of the grandest of the two-story Cloverdale homes. She could have graced a chair at the local country club, and with her astute mind she would have become a skillful bridge player. Instead, Helen Adele Friedman Blackshear became a certified teacher for thirty-five years. During all those years, she taught hundreds of students the rudiments of English composition and the skills needed for research, and she enthralled them with her love for literature, (both fiction and nonfiction) and especially with her love of poetry. I add that her students loved her and many became, like her, excellent teachers of literature.

In her lifetime, she was rewarded for her talent by being elected one of Alabama's poet laureates, selected by the Alabama Writers' Conclave, of which she was once the state president. She was twice the president of the historic Press and Authors' Club, and she had headed the state poetry society.

She and Sidney Lanier had common traits: each had three children, and each established their reputations as authors beginning in Montgomery, Alabama.

Separated by more than a hundred years, Helen Adele Friedman Blackshear and Sidney Clopton Lanier were also exceedingly different. While Helen's Jewish ancestors eventually became Presbyterians (probably the reason she was enrolled at Presbyterian-affiliated Agnes Scott College), Helen was active in the local Unitarian-Universalist church. Sidney Lanier was closely aligned with conservative Christian churches. Lanier's poor health left him debilitated, while Helen was always robust and enjoyed excellent health, even while she was long-caring for a very sick husband. Lanier only lived to be thirty-nine years old; Helen persevered until she was ninety-two.

While Sidney Lanier had family that instantly recognized his literary and musical talents, Helen was surrounded only by friends who shared her literary interests. She had only one literary cousin, Robert Longman, of whom Helen wrote her master's thesis at the University of Alabama, "Robert Longman, Belated Romanticist."

I like to think that as Helen's life drew to a close in that isolated cabin, once a part of the large Friedman estate, deep in the woods of Tuscaloosa County beside a trickling creek, that her last thoughts were of the Sidney Lanier biography and that she thought to herself the well-known part of his poem she so often read to her students with a strong voice and her own sweet smile:

As the marsh-hen secretly builds on the watery sod,
Behold I will build me a nest on the greatness of God:
I will fly in the greatness of God as the marsh-hen flies
In the freedom that fills all the space 'twixt the marsh and the skies:
By so many roots as the marsh-grass sends in the sod
I will heartily lay me a-hold on the greatness of God:
Oh, like the greatness of God is the greatness within
The range of the marshes, the liberal marshes of Glynn.

She lived and died as my idea of a gentle, compassionate, helpful, and humble woman of Greatness.

Editor's Note

AMANDA ADAMS

Helen Blackshear's capsule account of Sidney Lanier's life has a rich history of its own. Randall Williams, editor-in-chief of NewSouth Books, encouraged Blackshear (Alabama's poet laureate from 1995–99) to write the biography more than fourteen years ago. They had worked together on three previous books, and her anthology of verse by Alabama's poet laureates, *These I Would Keep*, was NewSouth's very first title when the new publishing house launched in 2000. The next year, Blackshear, by then in her nineties but still energetic and vital, asked Williams for suggestions for a new project. He proposed a modest biography of Sidney Lanier, and she jumped into research and writing.

She turned in a first draft of the project in 2002, unhappily about the time her health began to decline. The following summer, Mary Bridges, then an intern at NewSouth, worked on the project. Bridges, a Harvard literature graduate (and daughter of Ed Bridges, former director of the Alabama Department of Archives and History), helped Blackshear edit and polish a second draft, but it was not yet ready for publication when Blackshear died in November 2003.

Williams says he always wanted to finish the biography, but other projects interfered, and the Lanier bio stayed on the back burner. During the summer of 2012, I served as an editorial assistant at NewSouth Books. Williams asked me to work with the material we had in the files to prepare Blackshear's work for publication.

I discovered a lot of unretrievable or garbled computer files, a preliminary cover, and three separate drafts of the project on paper. Two of the drafts were remarkably similar, but the other was much different—the draft that Mary Bridges had worked on with Mrs. Blackshear. I studied the drafts and determined that repetition was not an issue; each draft referenced distinct events and information about Lanier's life, all of which were relevant. I thought the two versions complemented one another and could not bring myself to sacrifice one of the two. Instead, I pieced the two drafts together, readjusting and reworking the pieces of the story like the pieces of a jigsaw puzzle. For at least a week, my desk was littered with Post-it notes and multiple drafts covered in arrows and directions to myself.

Such revising of the drafts inevitably called for some rewriting of Blackshear's original text, as well as writing transitions between previously unconnected thoughts. I also updated the last section of the book regarding Lanier's current legacy. All edits, however, followed the lead of Blackshear's conversationally refined prose. In the final text of this volume, I feel confident that though Helen Blackshear has passed away, her words and voice live on, and through them, so does Sidney Lanier.

IT THEN TOOK STILL more time to get the book published, concurrent with a reissue of Blackshear's most significant collection of poetry, *Alabama Album*, which had gone out of print. Finally, in 2016, both books appeared.

Preface

HELEN BLACKSHEAR

I taught eleventh grade American literature for thirty years, and I always looked forward to our lesson on Sidney Lanier when I could read aloud "The Marshes of Glynn," which I consider one of the most exquisitely beautiful poems ever written. So when Randall Williams asked me if I would consider writing a book on Lanier's Montgomery years, I was glad to comply. I felt that I was revisiting an old and dear friend.

In the 1960s, my husband and I built a summer home on Joe's Bayou in Destin, Florida. There is a marshy area along the water's edge below the house that is the home of a big blue heron, a raccoon, and various other wild creatures. It is not as extensive, of course, as Lanier's Georgia marshes, but I cannot count the times his beautiful words have come to my mind as I watched the sunset from our porch. I would find myself quoting "By so many roots as the marsh-grass sends in the sod, I will heartily lay me a-hold on the greatness of God."

Lanier's two years in Montgomery are not even mentioned in most biographies of him, but they were important. He came here after his imprisonment during the Civil War, an ordeal that caused the tuberculosis that shortened his life. The clerk-ship he fulfilled in his uncle's Exchange Hotel gave him a resting period that restored his productivity. He loved Montgomery, and Montgomery loved him. Sidney Lanier deserves to have us remember and honor him.

Acknowledgments

The story of Sidney Lanier's Montgomery years comes mainly from his own pen, as both he and his brother Clifford were prolific letter writers. Thanks also are due to Sidney Lanier's many relations and admirers who painstakingly collected his letters and memorabilia in a prolonged effort to get him included in the Hall of Fame for Great Americans. This effort resulted in the twelve-volume *Centennial Edition of the Works of Sidney Lanier* at Johns Hopkins University, where Lanier had earned his greatest fame.

Thanks are due to Dr. Wayne DeLoach, who wrote about Lanier's teaching career in Prattville, Alabama, as well as to Mary Elizabeth Bridges for her helpful comments and critiques. Another important source of information about his Montgomery years is the biography *Sidney Lanier* by Edwin Mims, who was given access to all of Lanier's letters by his relatives, his wife, and his sons. These letters concern the part of his life that is the least known but that is very important in showing his devotion to his Southern roots.

Montgomery, Alabama, 2003

*Vanished in the
Unknown Shade*

Sidney Lanier's birthplace and boyhood home in Macon, Georgia. The cottage is open to the public for tours.

1

Young Life

Sidney Lanier was born in Macon, Georgia, on February 3, 1842, in a small cottage on High Street where his father, Robert Lanier, was a struggling young lawyer. His mother, Mary J. Anderson, was the daughter of a Virginia planter of Scotch-Irish ancestry. She was said to be devoutly religious and an accomplished pianist. Sidney was the firstborn child. His brother Clifford was born two years later and was soon followed by a sister, Gertrude. The two boys were devoted to each other, and both adored their sister who they called "Gussie."

Sidney could not remember a time when he could not play any musical instrument. When he was seven, he made a flute from a reed cut from the neighboring river bank, with six makeshift finger holes at the side. With this he imitated the trills of the song birds. Next year Santa brought him his first real flute, which he practiced constantly. He also organized an orchestra among his playmates. Meanwhile, he was discovering the joys of good literature in his father's library. He would develop and combine these two loves, literature and music, for all his life.

The people of Macon were noted for their hospitality, a continual round of musicals and evening parties, horseback and boat rides, piano and flute playing, singing, and impromptu cotillions and Virginia reels. The Lanier House, a hotel owned from 1844 to 1854 by Sterling Lanier, Sidney's grandfather, was the center of this social life.

Sidney Lanier lived in a room in Thalian Hall on the campus of Oglethorpe University, where he cultivated his interest in literature, joining his first in a succession of literary societies.

Sidney's father and grandfather were both cultured men with the typical literary tastes of gentlemen of the Old South. They were fond of Shakespeare, Joseph Addison, and Sir Walter Scott.

Sidney had begun his education studying law in his hometown, but his weak chest made him turn to literature instead. In January 1857, Lanier entered the sophomore class of Oglethorpe University near the sleepy town of Milledgeville, Georgia. This Presbyterian college confirmed his strong religious faith.

Sidney's major interest was still literature, but the teacher who had the greatest formative influence over him was James Woodrow, an Englishman who headed the science department. This teacher became Sidney Lanier's intimate friend.

Woodrow later wrote of his favorite pupil:

I . . . often took him to ramble with me, observing and

studying whatever we saw. . . . In these ways, and in listening frequently to his marvelous flute-playing, we were much together. We were both young and fond of study.[1]

Besides science, Lanier also studied the Greek and Latin classics, mastered mathematics, and became interested in philosophy. He was the only sophomore admitted to the secret literary society called the Thalians, of which he wrote to his father:

> I have derived more benefit from that, than any one of my collegiate studies. We meet together in a nice room, read compositions, declaim, and debate upon interesting subjects.[2]

His roommate, T. J. Newell, later wrote:

> I shall never forget those moonlight nights at old Oglethorpe, when, after study hours, we would crash up the stairway and get out on the cupola, making the night merry with music, song, and laughter. Sid would play upon his flute like one inspired, while the rest of us would listen in solemn silence.[3]

Sidney's younger brother Clifford followed him to Oglethorpe University and soon also became a member of the prestigious literary society. He roomed with Sidney, and the devotion between the brothers was deep and constant, almost like that of twins. They shared a love of poetry, collaborated on a number of poems, and even planned to publish a volume of poems to be written jointly. When apart they kept in touch with long letters. Sidney's letters to Clifford often began "my darling Clifford" and were full of advice and encouragement.

In September 1865, he wrote to Clifford:

I think you will make a splendid writer, if you practice. Keep a small blank-book in your pocket and note on it every idea, whether fantastical, comic, or poetical, that occurs to you. You will find them all come to use; it is to me an indispensable thing, and has been the practice of all authors.[4]

In July 1860, Sidney graduated at the head of his class. There followed a month's idyllic visit with some twenty family members at his grandfather's vacation home in the Tennessee mountains, where he enjoyed the life of the Old South at its best just before it vanished in the cataclysm of the Civil War.

After a year of tutoring at Oglethorpe University, Lanier formed the practical plan of studying at a German university, probably Heidelberg, as a preliminary to a professorship in an American college. The outbreak of war wrecked these fine ambitions.

To ʏᴏᴜɴɢ ᴍᴇɴ ʟɪᴋᴇ Lanier, the Southern cause was one of resistance to despotism and fanaticism, of the protection of home. Soon after finishing the year's work at Oglethorpe, he volunteered for service and went to Virginia where he joined the Macon Volunteers, and he was soon followed by his brother Clifford.

They participated in the Seven Days' fighting around Richmond, marching through drenching rain over torn and swampy roads. Following a gunboat fight on the James River and a rest period at Petersburg, the two brothers were transferred to the signal corps, considered to be the most efficient organization in the Confederate army. During their two years as scouts, they were in constant danger of being captured.

In August 1864, Sidney was transferred to Wilmington, North Carolina, where he became a signal officer on a blockade runner, a service of keen excitement, demanding a clear head

Young Sidney Lanier, in the beginning of his artistic career, could have no idea of his troublesome life ahead. He would contract tuberculosis while imprisoned at Point Lookout Prison in Maryland and struggle with it for the rest of his short life.

and iron nerves. On November 2, 1864, his boat, *The Lucy,* was captured in the Gulf Stream en route to Bermuda. Sidney Lanier was taken to Point Lookout Prison in Maryland where he spent four dreary months. Lanier always attributed his breakdown in health to this prison.

Montgomery's well-loved Judge Walter B. Jones described Lanier's confinement in a gloomy prison ship in his newspaper column in the *Montgomery Advertiser,* "Off the Bench":

> After four months' imprisonment at Point Lookout a number of young soldiers were being transferred to Fortress Monroe. The season was winter and the cold was penetrating. Many were sick and in need of attention. Apparently near death, the subject of this sketch lay in a corner of the hold, difficult to reach on account of the crowded conditions of the floor. A Southern woman from Alabama looked in upon the men with motherly sympathy. Suddenly she saw and recognized

Clifford Lanier, Sidney's younger brother, spent the majority of his adult life in Montgomery. He followed in the footsteps of his older brother and was a novelist and poet in his own right. His novel, Thorn-Fruit, *was published in 1867, the same year as Sidney's* Tiger-Lilies.

the youth away off in a distant corner. Picking her way to his side, she strove in vain to rouse him from his heavy stupor.

With the consent of the officer in charge, she determined to have him carried to her quarters, where she could minister to him. The ranks of men lay so close together that it was impossible for stretcher-bearers to get to him, therefore his young comrades nearest to him lifted him gently and passed him on to the arms of the soldiers next in the row. They, themselves sick, wearied, discouraged, sighed as they touched his clammy hands. Sadly they watched the bearers carry the body aloft to the quarters of the lady, who had a special passport to travel to Richmond.[5]

Saved by her careful nursing, Sidney Lanier was finally able to walk home to Macon. After his painful journey through the Carolinas, Sidney was ill for two months. While there he helped his father and his sister, Gussie, care for his mother, who was seriously ill.

Clifford had not been imprisoned with Sidney, as he had escaped to Cuba after the blockade at Wilmington. Clifford arrived in Macon just a few days before his mother's death from consumption. The two brothers collaborated in writing a mourning poem.

Clifford then accepted a job in Montgomery as a clerk in the Exchange Hotel, which had been founded by his grandfather and was jointly managed by his uncles Will Lanier and Abram Watt, who had married his aunt Jane Lanier.

Sidney, meanwhile, began work as a tutor on a large plantation near Macon. With many classes each day and failing health, he endured the boring monotony of the schoolroom.

THE ONE BRIGHT EPISODE in these hardworking days was his renewed friendship with Mary Day, a lovely young lady whose father was a prominent businessman in Macon.

Sidney had met Mary during the war in the spring of 1863 while he was on a two-week furlough in Macon. They had been introduced by Mrs. Clement C. Clay, wife of the senator. Since 1851, Mary had been studying music in New York and living with cultured people in Saratoga and West Point. She shared Sidney's love of poetry and music and was destined to play an important role in his life.

2

THE MONTGOMERY YEARS

By the fall of 1865, Sidney was desperate for a job. Clifford had left Oglethorpe University without finishing because of his health and was then a clerk at the Exchange Hotel in Montgomery.

Sidney confided his troubles to Clifford on November 25, 1865:

> My destitute condition is the Death's Head at all my feasts. It drives me hard, night and day towards the grave. Two months more, like the two months gone, will put me yonder beside Mother. . . . Who else will be employed by Uncle Abe in the Office, besides yourself? If he has engaged no one, couldn't I get it?[6]

To Sidney's great relief, Clifford replied with the offer of a clerkship at the Exchange Hotel "with such a salary . . . as would enable you to support most comfortably yourself and another."[7]

Sidney arrived in Montgomery in December 1865 to an enthusiastic welcome. Both in and around Montgomery, Sidney was surrounded by loving family members. His sister Gussie was spending the winter with her grandparents in Robinson Springs (near present-day Millbrook), only twenty miles north of Montgomery. Besides spending much time visiting his grandparents at their country home in Robinson Springs, Sidney also enjoyed helping them celebrate their golden wedding anniversary and wrote a poem for the occasion.

Both Abram Watt and Will Lanier, managers of the Exchange Hotel, were in Montgomery during Sidney's time there. Will was also manager of the Grand Hotel in Mobile, but it was closed for the season.

Sidney's and Clifford's work at the Exchange Hotel was made congenial by their Aunt Jane Watt, who had in more prosperous times before the war traveled much in the North and been friends with Jefferson Davis and Alexander Stephens. Also they found pleasure in social affairs with the Cloptons and Ligons, former owners of large cotton plantations.

For the first time in his troubled adult life, Sidney found himself relieved of financial worries and surrounded by admiring friends who appreciated his talents. His duties as a clerk were not arduous and left him time to write poems and to play his flute. Another of Judge Walter B. Jones's newspaper columns relates that when Lanier played the flute in the late evenings, hotel guests

EXCHANGE HOTEL,

MONTGOMERY, ALA.

____

THE ONLY FIRST-CLASS HOTEL IN THE CITY.

____

WATT & LANIER,

J. D. BEALE, Chief Clerk.   Proprietors.

An advertisement for the Lanier family's Exchange Hotel in Montgomery. Sidney's grandfather founded the hotel, Sidney's uncles managed the hotel's operations, and both Sidney and Clifford worked there as clerks.

would come down to the lobby in their nightclothes to listen to his golden notes.

He and Clifford were both working on novels—his brother's was called *Thorn-Fruit*—and hoped to find publishers in New York. Sidney wrote his father in July 1866:

> Two or three of every seven evenings are spent in making music for, and knowing the good people here. I have changed somewhat my reclusive habits and, without dissipating, am striving to be sociable. . . . We have a Literary Society, which is just beginning to flourish finely. Upon the invitation of some of the members, Cliff and I have joined it, and have already taken some stand. I made a speech last night, which has brought out several congratulations.[8]

At this time Mary Day, now his fiancée, was still in Macon. The following year when Clifford became engaged to his pretty cousin, Wilhelmina Clopton, he and Sidney discussed the possibility of a double wedding in the spring, but this did not happen.

DESPITE HIS WARM RECEPTION in Montgomery, Sidney found the once-prosperous town sadly changed. In a reply to a letter from Milton Northrup, a Northern friend, he wrote:

> I thank you, more than I can well express, for your kind letter. . . . It takes away the sulphur and the blood-flecks, and drowns out the harsh noises of battle. . . . I despair of giving you any idea of the mortal stagnation which paralyzes all business here. . . . Everything is dreamy, and drowsy, and drone-y. The trees stand like statues; and even when a breeze comes, the leaves flutter and dangle idly about, as if with a languid protest against all disturbance of their perfect rest. The mocking-birds

absolutely refuse to sing before twelve o'clock at night, when the
air is somewhat cooled. . . . I begin to have serious thoughts of
emigrating to your country, so that I may live a little. There's
not enough attrition of mind on mind here, to bring out any
sparks from a man.[9]

Some members of Lanier's family "who used to roll in wealth,"
he continues, "are every day with their own hands plowing the
little patch of ground which the war has left them, while their
wives do the cooking and washing."[10]

In spite of the sad state of business, Sidney contrived to oc-
cupy himself pleasantly. In September 1866, he wrote to Gussie:

I have just returned from Tuskegee, where I spent a pleasant week. . . . Indeed, they were all so good and so kind to me,

This 1857 engraving from Harper's Weekly *demonstrates what
Montgomery must have looked like during Lanier's time there.
The scene looks up Dexter Avenue toward the capitol building.
The Exchange Hotel was less than half a mile from the capitol.*

Photograph of the Exchange Hotel. Lanier's time in Montgomery and at the Exchange Hotel was characterized by fellowship, music, and merriment with friends, family, and hotel guests.

and the fair cousins were so beautiful, that I came back feeling as if I had been in a week's dream of fairyland.[11]

To keep in touch with the world of letters, Lanier subscribed to the *Round Table*, a New York weekly that was sympathetic to the South and that the *New York Times* said had "the genius and learning and brilliancy of the higher order of London weeklies."[12] Lanier was impressed by an editorial on July 7, 1866, which proclaimed:

The people of the South are our brothers, bone of our bone and flesh of our flesh. They have courage, integrity, honor, patriotism, and all the manly virtues as well as ourselves. . . . Can we realize that our duty now is to heal, not to punish?[13]

TIGER-LILIES.

A NOVEL.

BY

SIDNEY LANIER.

For mine is but an humble muse,
And owning but a little art
To lull with song an aching heart,
And give to earthly Love his dues.
Tennyson

NEW YORK:
PUBLISHED BY HURD AND HOUGHTON,
459 BROOME STREET.
1867.

The title page of the first edition of Lanier's only novel. He devoted much of his time in Montgomery to working on it.

After Sidney Lanier's novel, *Tiger-Lilies*, was published in 1867, a review of it in the *Round Table* refers to Lanier as "the author of some quaint and graceful verses published from time to time in the *Round Table*. His novel goes a long way to confirm the good opinion which his poems suggested. . . . His errors seem to be entirely errors of youth and in the right direction. Exuberance is more easily corrected than sterility."[14]

Although Edwin Mims describes Lanier's novel as a failure, "the plot badly managed and the work strikingly uneven,"[15] there are many interesting passages, such as this one describing a character's playing of the flute:

> It is like walking in the woods, amongst wild flowers, just before you go into some vast cathedral. For the flute seems to me to be peculiarly the woods-instrument: it speaks the gloss of green leaves or the pathos of bare branches; it calls up the strange mosses that are under dead leaves; it breathes of wild plants that hide and oak fragrances that vanish; it expresses to me the natural magic of music.[16]

Music was as important to Lanier as poetry, perhaps more important, and the Montgomery years were full of music. Besides the flute, Sidney and Clifford collaborated on guitars and clarinets. Sidney was also an organist for the Presbyterian Church. According to his father, "It is as natural for [Sidney] to land in an organ-loft as it is for a bird to hop into a tree."[17]

Before he and Clifford left for New York in the fall, hoping to publish their novels, they gave a famous farewell party on a Sunday night in the Exchange Hotel that no participant would ever forget. The guests were regaled with violins, guitars, clarionettes, and, of course, Sidney's flute. The hilarity was so great that their uncle Abram Watt, the manager of the hotel, was forced to object to the noise. Later Sidney wrote his aunt Jane Watt: "Do apologize to Uncle Abram for the noise, it being our first offence."[18]

On a return visit to Montgomery on August 10, 1867, Sidney wrote Mary:

> I am already famous here in Montgomery, and the shower of kind words, of congratulation, of compliments to my little poems (all of which have been republished here) is become even painful.[19]

Sidney's two years in Montgomery gave him a restful time to slowly recover his strength. He read avidly and talked about books with congenial friends. He had leisure to experiment with new forms of poetry, although no important poems are attributed to this period. He confessed his own defects as a poet—verboseness, choosing words for sound rather than meaning.

The Montgomery period prepared him for the fame he would later receive as one of the two most important postwar poets in the South, second only to Edgar Allan Poe, whom Lanier greatly admired.

Although Lanier's achievements in literature and music fill many volumes in the library of Johns Hopkins University in Baltimore, Maryland, where he earned his greatest fame, he won the devotion of Montgomery, Alabama, when he called it Home.

3

Journey to an Artistic Career

On August 15, 1867, Sidney wrote Mary, then still his fiancée, about a proposed Male and Female Academy in Prattville, Alabama, and the prospect of his becoming its principal. Two weeks later he became the unanimous choice of the board of trustees and was soon busily selecting textbooks and acquiring two assistants, a talented young language instructor, Mr. McWilliams, and an older woman, Mrs. Morgan, for the primary department.

He spent the winter in this small manufacturing town working "from sun up to sun down."[20] But he wrote his father, "Not even the wide-mouthed, villainous-nosed, tallow-faced drudgeries of my eighty-fold life can squeeze the sentiment out of me."[21]

When a Northern friend asked Sidney to accompany him to Germany, he replied:

> Your trip-to-Europe invitation finds me all thirsty to go with you; but, alas, how little do you know of our wretched poverties and distresses here,—that you ask me such a thing. . . . It spoils our dream of Germany, ruthlessly. I've been presiding over eighty-six scholars, in a large Academy at Prattville, Alabama. . . . The labor difficulties, with the recent poor price of cotton, conspire to make the pay very slim. I think your people can have no idea of the slow terrors with which this winter has invested our life in the South.[22]

Lanier was reportedly a gifted and inspiring teacher, but the perilous plight of the Reconstruction South militated against the success of the school. On September 29, 1867, Lanier wrote Mary from Prattville, "The terrible decline in the price of cotton and the consequent 'blues' of the planters will probably keep many away."[23]

Lanier's family, like many, was impoverished. Sidney's few poems of this period are full of bitterness at the poverty and despair of the prostrate South. In a poem called "The Raven Days," he expressed his feelings:

Our hearths are gone out and our hearts are broken,
    And but the ghosts of homes to us remain.
And ghastly eyes and hollow sighs give token
    From friend to friend of an unspoken pain.
. . .
O Raven days, dark Raven days of sorrow,
    Will ever any warm light come again?
Will ever the lit mountains of To-morrow
    Begin to gleam athwart the mournful plain?[24]

DESPITE LANIER'S GRIEF OVER the excesses of Reconstruction, he did not blame the blacks for everything. He wrote to his father in 1868 while he was teaching in Prattville:

> There are strong indications here of much bad feeling between the whites and blacks, especially those engaged in the late row at this place; and I have fears . . . that some indiscretion of the more thoughtless among the whites may plunge us into bloodshed. The whites have no organization at all, and the affair would be a mere butchery.[25]

These are not the words of a racist. Later, in a public address in 1870 for the Confederate Memorial in Macon, he showed that he had risen above all bitterness and prejudice: "Today we are here for love and not for hate. Today we are here for harmony and not for discord. Today we are risen immeasurably above all vengeance."[26] The spirit of the address is like that seen in the letters of Robert E. Lee, one of Lanier's heroes. Many Southerners, like Lee, were ready to forget the bitterness and prejudice of the war.

In October he had to discharge his assistant teacher and borrow money from his father to pay Mrs. Morgan, who was resigning. On November 15th, he wrote his father, "Planters hold their cotton, and my collections come slowly."[27] Next year he wrote his Aunt Jane Lanier Watt that his school had become smaller and that "people come to me almost with tears in their eyes, and represent their fearful impoverishment which prevents them from sending children to school."[28]

Early in 1868 Lanier himself was forced to resign. To make matters worse, the first serious symptoms of tuberculosis appeared in the form of a severe hemorrhage from the lungs. He was confined to his bed for several months and never fully recovered.

Meanwhile, he and Mary Day had married, and she had joined him in Prattville. When they met in 1863 in Macon, Mary had been engaged to Fred Andrew for several years, but this did not prevent Lanier's writing to her and her enthusiastic responses. With Mary engaged to Fred, Sidney courted Virginia Hankins while he and Clifford were stationed with the Confederate signal corps (2nd Battalion, Macon Volunteers) at Burwell's Bay, Virginia, from May 1863 to October 1864. Virginia Hankins's family owned Bacon's Castle in Surry County, and Sidney and Clifford visited there often and were friends of the family. Sidney proposed marriage to Virginia but she did not accept. Poor Fred was eventually thrown overboard, and Mary and Sidney were married on December 21, 1867. Their marriage was apparently one of mutual lifelong devotion.

A poem written to Mary shortly after their marriage shows his love for her. It is a parody of Chaucer, whom he admired.

Hire eyen grey as bodyglass;
Hire mouth ful smale, and thereto soft and red;
But sikerly she had a fayre forehed.
It was almost a spanne brod, I trowe.

Of smale corall about hire arm she bare
A pair of bedes, gauded all with grene;
And thereon heng a broche of gold ful shene,
On which was first ywritten a crowned *A*,
And after, *Amor Vincit Omnia*.[29]

Lanier's biographer Edwin Mims wrote:

It was an idyllic marriage, which the poet thought a rich compensation for all the other perfect gifts which Providence denied him. She was a sufferer like himself, but her accuracy and alertness of mind, her rare appreciation of music, and her deep divining of his own powers, made her the ideal wife of the poet.[30]

A young Mary Day in 1865, two years before her marriage to Sidney Lanier.

Their residence in Prattville, however, was not as idyllic as their marriage. The small, industrial town ridden with the despair of Reconstruction did not provide the comforts to which both Mary and Sidney were accustomed in Macon and elsewhere.

Needing to earn more money to support his family, Lanier decided to go into his father's law office. He spent 1868 studying for the Georgia bar and joined the firm in 1869. His advantages were good, since his father and uncle were among the oldest lawyers in Macon and had a large practice.

A fellow lawyer, Chancellor Walter B. Hill of the University of Georgia, later wrote of Lanier's legal experience:

> The greater part of his work consisted in the examination of titles. . . . One cannot imagine work that is more dry-as-dust in its character. . . . When I came into the firm I had occasion frequently to examine the letter-press copybook in which Lanier's "abstracts" or reports upon the title had been copied. Not only were the books themselves models of neatness, but all his work in the examination of titles showed the utmost thoroughness, patience, and fidelity. . . . I have often keenly felt the contrast between such toil and that for which Lanier's genius fitted him.[31]

In November 1872, Lanier went to San Antonio, Texas, in search of health. It was on this visit that he finally resolved to devote himself to an artist's career. This decision was influenced by the enthusiastic reception his flute playing received after performing before the Maennerchor. This group of about seventeen Germans met at the singing-table each Wednesday night to practice "noble old German full-voiced *lied*."[32]

"After the second song," Lanier wrote, "I was called on to play, and lifted my poor old flute in air with tumultuous, beating

heart; for I had no confidence in that or in myself. . . . To my ut-
ter astonishment, I was perfect master of the instrument. . . . I
commanded and the blessed notes obeyed me, and when I had
finished, amid a storm of applause. . . . My heart, which was hurt
greatly when I went into the music-room, came forth from the
holy bath of concords greatly refreshed, strengthened, and qui-
eted."[33] Reaffirmed in his talents, Lanier "went from San Antonio
in April 1873, with the fixed purpose of giving the remainder of
his life to music and poetry."[34]

His father wrote, begging him to change his mind, but Lanier's
reply was a declaration of independence:

> How can I settle myself down to be a third-rate strug-
> gling lawyer for the balance of my little life, as long as there
> is certainty almost absolute that I can do some other thing so
> much better? Several persons, from whose judgment in such
> matters there can be no appeal, have told me, for instance, that
> I am the greatest flute player in the world; and several others,
> of equally authoritative judgment, have given me an almost
> equal encouragement to work with my pen.[35]

Lanier then went to New York for three months of hard
work to perfect himself on the flute. He would be satisfied only
with the judgment of Dr. Leopold Damrosch, conductor of the
Philharmonic Society.

On the way to New York, Lanier stopped in Baltimore where
Asger Hamerik was trying to get the Peabody Institute to estab-
lish an orchestra. Hamerik was impressed with Lanier's playing
and invited him to become first flute in the projected orchestra.

Lanier wrote enthusiastically to Mary:

> It is therefore a possibility . . . that I may be first flute in

the Peabody Orchestra, on a salary of . . . $200 a month, and so . . . we might dwell in the beautiful city, among the great libraries, and midst of the music, the religion, and the art that we love—and I could write my books and be the man I wish to be.[36]

Lanier's hope of bringing his family to Baltimore did not come to fruition as soon as he might have hoped. He could not afford to bring them to Baltimore until 1877 and had to content himself with annual summer visits to his beloved homeland.

He hated his separation from his wife and sons and spoke of himself as "an exile from [my] dear Land, which is always

The Peabody Institute played a major role in Lanier's life during his eight years in Baltimore. He was first flute in the Peabody Orchestra and later planned a series of lectures that led to his appointment at Johns Hopkins University.

the land where my loved ones are."[42]

In his home life Lanier was at his best, and with his children his spirit of fun-making was ever present. As he writes to Mary in January 1875:

> I do so long for one hearty romp with my boys again! Kiss them most fervently for me. . . . Let us try and teach them, dear wife, that it is only the small soul that ever cherishes bitterness; for the climate of a large and loving heart is too warm for that frigid plant. Let us lead them to love everything in the world.[43]

DURING THE WINTER OF 1873 and the next one, Lanier wrote no poetry, giving almost his entire time to music and taking every opportunity to play with the best musicians.

The director of the orchestra, who had been a pupil of Hans von Bülow, said of Lanier:

> His human nature was like an enchanted instrument, a magic flute. . . . In his hands the flute no longer remained a mere material instrument, but was transformed into a voice that set heavenly harmonies into vibration.[37]

He also won high praise from his hero Dr. Damrosch, who said he played "Wind Song" like an artist, and that "he was greatly astonished and pleased with the poetry of the piece and the enthusiasm of its rendering."[38]

Still, he wrote, "I am not yet an artist, though, on the flute. The technique of the instrument has many depths which I had not thought of before."[39]

Lanier became interested in the science of music and its history, giving biological sketches of the English musicians of Shakespeare's age for a class to which he was lecturing at the Peabody

Institute. Lanier associated nature, music, and poetry with each other. He saw music as he heard poetry. He also believed in the religious value of music, that it was "a gospel whereof the people are in great need. . . . Music will be one of the redeemers of the people from crass commercialism."[40]

Lanier was disgusted at times with the Bohemianism and loose moral life of the men in the orchestra, once giving vent to his feelings in a letter to Mary: "Dash these fellows, they are utterly given over to heathenism, prejudice, and beer."[41]

LANIER HAD A GREAT sense of humor, as is shown in his enjoyment of the Negro and the "Florida Cracker" in his dialect poems like "Uncle Jim's Baptist Revival Hymn." He was always open minded and a close student of current events though he spoke out strongly against the materialism of the nineteenth century. He had a remarkable power for making friends and a tremendous personal magnetism.

At a party in Baltimore in the winter of 1874, Lanier was interviewed by one of the female guests as part of the entertainment, as was popular at the time. His written replies illuminate his character and ideals:

Favorite names, male and female?
    Clifford and Mary.
Favorite musicians?
    Schumann, Wagner, Beethoven, Chopin.
Favorite poets?
    Shakspere, Chaucer, Lucretius, Robert Browning.
Favorite poetesses?
    Elizabeth Browning, George Eliot.
Favorite prose authors?
    William Hamilton, Thomas Browne, Carlyle, Richter.

Favorite occupation?
Teaching: either by poems, by music, or by lectures.
What is your idea of happiness?
A table with pen and paper, under a big oak, in
early summer: wife seated where I can see her every
second: three boys rolling on the grass: a mountain in
the distance and a certainty that my article won't be
declined.[44]

In November 1875, Lanier spent a week at the Parker House in Boston visiting Charlotte Cushman, an intimate and talented elderly friend who was near death from an incurable illness. During this week he "spent two 'delightful afternoons' with [James Russell] Lowell and [Henry] Longfellow." Later Lowell wrote of Lanier: "He was not only a man of genius with a rare gift for the happy word, but had in him qualities that won affection and commanded respect."[45]

By the summer of 1876, Lanier had thus established himself as a man of letters. He had not only written poetry but had also found a place among a group of artists that recognized the value of his work and the charm of his personality.

4

A Year of Poetry

Sidney Lanier has been called "the first important postwar Southern writer, a spokesman not of regional but of national vision."[46]

The year 1877 was one of Lanier's most productive, in spite of his increasing illness. Lanier wrote:

> I am taken with a poem pretty nearly every day, and have to content myself with making a note of its train of thought on the back of whatever letter is in my coat-pocket. . . . I am trying with all my might to put off composition of all sorts until some approach to the certainty of next week's dinner shall remove this remnant of haste, and leave me that repose which ought to fill the artist's firmament while he is creating.[47]

He found the subject closest to his heart when he began to write of the beloved Georgia scenes of his boyhood. On a visit to Georgia in the summer, he enjoyed the natural scenery of Macon and was struck with the beauty of the cornfields outside the town. This inspired his first important poem, "Corn," written in August 1874. The poem was published in 1875 in *Lippincott's Magazine.*

"Corn" is distinctly Southern, showing the poet's love of the forest, the pathos of the deserted fields, and the thriftless and negligent farmer. Foreshadowing the Southern Agrarian Movement in the early twentieth century, Lanier believed the redemption of

Though Lanier was a beardless, spiritual-looking youth in his Montgomery years, pictures in his later life show him as heavily bearded—somewhat resembling Stonewall Jackson.

the country would come through the development of agriculture, not the big plantations of the old regime, but the large number of small farms with diversified products.

After his early success with "Corn" he wrote "The Symphony" and "Psalm of the West," which were fairly well received, but he reached his most admired and musical perfection in "The Song of the Chattahoochee":

The Song of the Chattahoochee

Out of the hills of Habersham,
　　Down the valleys of Hall,
I hurry amain to reach the plain,
Run the rapid and leap the fall,
Spin at the rock and together again,
Accept my bed, or narrow or wide,
And flee from folly on every side
With a lover's pain to attain the plain
　　Far from the hills of Habersham,
　　Far from the valleys of Hall.

All down the hills of Habersham,
　　All through the valleys of Hall,
The rushes cried, *Abide, abide,*
The willful waterweeds held me thrall,
The laving laurel turned my tide,
The ferns and the fondling grass said *Stay,*
The dewberry dipped for to work delay,
And the little reeds sighed, *Abide, abide,*
　　Here in the hills of Habersham,
　　Here in the valleys of Hall.

High o'er the hills of Habersham,
Veiling the valleys of Hall,
The hickory told me manifold
Fair tales of shade, the poplar tall
Wrought me her shadowy self to hold,
The chestnut, the oak, the walnut, the pine,
Overleaning, with flickering meaning and sign,
Said, *Pass not, so cold, these manifold*
Deep shades of the hills of Habersham,
These glades in the valleys of Hall.

And oft in the hills of Habersham,
And oft in the valleys of Hall,
The white quartz shone, and the smooth brook-stone
Did bar me of passage with friendly brawl,
And many a luminous jewel lone
—Crystals clear or a-cloud with mist,
Ruby, garnet, and amethyst—
Made lures with the lights of streaming stone
In the clefts of the hills of Habersham,
In the beds of the valleys of Hall.

But oh, not the hills of Habersham,
And oh, not the valleys of Hall
Avail: I am fain for to water the plain.
Downward the voices of Duty call—
Downward, to toil and be mixed with the main;
The dry fields burn, and the mills are to turn,
And a myriad flowers mortally yearn,
And the lordly main from beyond the plain
Calls o'er the hills of Habersham,
Calls through the valleys of Hall.[48]

In a video documentary, *Sidney Lanier, Poet of the Marshes,*
Jack Debellis claims:

> To legions of students who have memorized it, the poem
> has proved unforgettable for its meter, rhyme, and clashing
> tone colors, partly due to the wealth of musical devices used
> to create a fluid movement. . . . The playfulness of the poet
> perfectly mirrors the playfulness of the river.[49]

Lanier especially loved Anglo-Saxon poetry, and his best
poems show the influence of its rhythms. Lanier's idea of the
music in poetry is well illustrated in his poem, "An Evening Song":

An Evening Song

Look off, dear love, across the shallow sands
    And mark yon meeting of the sun and sea,
How long they kiss in sight of all the lands.
    Ah! longer, longer we.

Now in the sea's red vintage melts the sun,
    As Egypt's pearl dissolved in rosy wine,
And Cleopatra night drinks all. 'Tis done,
    Love, lay thine hand in mine.

Come forth, sweet stars, and comfort heaven's heart;
    Glimmer, ye waves, round else unlighted sands.
O night! divorce our sun and sky apart,
    Never our lips, our hands.[50]

THROUGHOUT HIS LIFE, LANIER maintained a deep religious faith
that is evident in all his poems, especially "A Ballad of Trees and

the Master." This is a lovely religious poem that has been set to music and is a favorite with church choirs:

A Ballad of Trees and the Master

Into the woods my Master went,
Clean forspent, forspent.
Into the woods my Master came,
Forspent with love and shame.
But the olives they were not blind to Him,
The little gray leaves were kind to Him:
The thorn tree had a mind to Him
When into the woods He came.

Out of the woods my Master went,
And He was well content.
Out of the woods by Master came,
Content with death and shame.
When Death and Shame would woo Him last,
From under the trees they drew Him last:
'Twas on a tree they slew Him—last
When out of the woods He came.[51]

Unquestionably the greatest of Lanier's poems and one of the truly great American poems is "The Marshes of Glynn," a poem in which the melody corresponds to the exalted thought. It must be read aloud to be appreciated. The music and the repetitions of the words "gloom" and "Glynn" make it an intimate personal experience.

It has the spirituality of Emerson and the healing power of the woods, combined with the expression of man's faith.

The Marshes of Glynn

Glooms of the live oaks, beautiful-braided and woven
With intricate shades of the vines that myriad-cloven
Clamber the forks of the multiform boughs—
  Emerald twilights—
  Virginal shy lights,
Wrought of the leaves to allure to the whisper of vows,
When lovers pace timidly down through the green colonnades
Of the dim sweet woods, of the dear dark woods,
  Of the heavenly woods and glades,
That run to the radiant marginal sand-beach within
  The wide sea-marshes of Glynn;—
Beautiful glooms, soft dusks in the noonday fire,—
Wildwood privacies, closets of lone desire,
Chamber from chamber parted with wavering arras of leaves,—
Cells for the passionate pleasure of prayer to the soul that grieves,
Pure with a sense of the passing of saints through the wood,
Cool for the dutiful weighing of ill with good;—

O braided dusks of the oak and woven shades of the vine,
While the riotous noonday sun of the June day long did shine
Ye held me fast in your heart and I held you fast in mine;
But now when the noon is no more, and riot is rest,
And the sun is a-wait at the ponderous gate of the West,
And the slant yellow beam down the wood-aisle doth seem
Like a lane into heaven that leads from a dream,—
Ay, now, when my soul all day hath drunken the soul of the oak,
And my heart is at ease from men, and the wearisome sound
of the stroke
  Of the scythe of time, and the trowel of trade is low,
  And belief overmasters doubt, and I know that I know,

And my spirit is grown to a lordly great compass within,
That the length and the breadth and the sweep of the marshes of
Glynn
Will work me no fear like the fear they have wrought me of yore
When length was fatigue, and when breadth was but bitterness
sore,
And when terror and shrinking and dreary unnamable pain
Drew over me out of the merciless miles of the plain—

Oh, now, unafraid, I am fain to face
 The vast sweet visage of space.
To the edge of the wood I am drawn, I am drawn,
Where the gray beach glimmering runs, as a belt of the dawn,
 For a mete and a mark
 To the forest dark:—
  So:
Affable live-oak, leaning low—
Thus—with your favor—soft, with a reverent hand,
(Not lightly touching your person, Lord of the land!)
Bending your beauty aside, with a step I stand
On the firm-packed sand,
  Free
By a world of marsh that borders a world of sea.

Sinuous southward and sinuous northward the shimmering band
 Of the sand beach fastens the fringe of the marsh to the
 folds of the land.
Inward and outward to northward and southward the beach-
lines linger and curl
As a silver-wrought garment that clings to and follows the firm
sweet limbs of a girl.
Vanishing, swerving, evermore curving again into sight,

Softly the sand-beach wavers away to a dim gray looping of light.
And what if behind me to westward the wall of the woods
stands high?
The world lies east: how ample, the marsh and the sea and the sky!
A league and a league of marsh-grass, waist-high, broad in the
blade,
Green, and all of a height, and unflecked with a light or a shade,
Stretch leisurely off, in a pleasant plain,
To the terminal blue of the main.

Oh what is abroad in the marsh and the terminal sea?
    Somehow my soul seems suddenly free
From the weighing of fate and the sad discussion of sin,
By the length and the breadth and the sweep of the marshes of
Glynn.

Ye marshes, how candid and simple and nothing withholding
and free
Ye publish yourselves to the sky and offer yourselves to the sea!
Tolerant plains, that suffer the sea and the rains and the sun,
Ye spread and span like the catholic man who hath mightily won
God out of knowledge and good out of infinite pain
And sight out of blindness and purity out of a stain.

As the marsh-hen secretly builds on the watery sod,
Behold I will build me a nest on the greatness of God:
I will fly in the greatness of God as the marsh-hen flies
In the freedom that fills all the space 'twixt the marsh and the
skies:
By so many roots as the marsh-grass sends in the sod
I will heartily lay me a-hold on the greatness of God:
Oh, like to the greatness of God is the greatness within

The range of the marshes, the liberal marshes of Glynn.

And the sea lends large, as the marsh: lo, out of his plenty the sea
Pours fast: full soon the time of the flood-tide must be:
Look how the grace of the sea doth go
About and about through the intricate channels that flow
    Here and there
      Everywhere,
Till his waters have flooded the uttermost creeks and the low-
lying lanes,
And the marsh is meshed with a million veins,
That like as with rosy and silvery essences flow
In the rose-and-silver evening glow,
     Farewell, my lord Sun!
The creeks overflow: a thousand rivulets run
'Twixt the roots of the sod; the blades of the marsh-grass stir;
Passeth a hurrying sound of wings that westward whirr,
Passeth, and all is still; and the currents cease to run;
And the sea and the marsh are one.

How still the plains of the waters be!
The tide is in his ecstasy;
The tide is at his highest height;
    And it is night.

And now from the Vast of the Lord will the waters of sleep
Roll in on the souls of men,
But who will reveal to our waking ken
The forms that swim and the shapes that creep
    Under the waters of sleep?
And I would I could know what swimmeth below when the
tide comes in

On the length and the breadth of the marvelous marshes of
Glynn.[52]

It is fitting that the state of Georgia has built a beautiful,
soaring bridge across the marshes, and it bears the name of the
poet who so beautifully described them.

*The Sidney Lanier Bridge crosses the South Brunswick River in
Glynn County, Georgia. The cable-stayed suspension bridge looks
out across the marshes the poet loved so much.*

5

A Lasting Legacy

After a year of inspiration in his poetry, Lanier found himself still in need of a livelihood. He began searching for a position—a lecturer at Johns Hopkins, a position in the Peabody Library, or a government job in Washington. Sadly, he was unable to secure even a clerkship, and he mourned: "Altogether, it seems as if there wasn't any place for me in this world."[53]

This mood soon passed, however, and his usual optimism returned. In 1877 he moved his family to a small four-room flat in Baltimore, from which he wrote his friend Gibson Peacock:

> I have also coaxed my landlord into all manner of outlays for damp walls, cold bathrooms, and other like matters. . . . I have had a Xmas tree for the youngsters, have looked up a cheap school for Harry and Sidney, have discharged my daily duties as first flute of the Peabody Orchestra, [and] have written a couple of poems.[54]

In the winter of 1877–78, with the aid of the Peabody Library, Lanier also began an intensive study of literature. He had impressed Paul Hamilton Haynes earlier with his thorough knowledge of Chaucer and the Elizabethan poets. Now he began to study them in a more scholarly way.

One of the librarians said:

He usually came in the morning, occupying the same seat at the end of the table, where he worked until lunchtime, so absorbed with his studies that he scarcely ever raised his eyes to notice anything around him.[55]

As an outcome of this study, Lanier planned a series of lectures on English literature by prominent scholars. The Peabody lectures led to Lanier's appointment as a lecturer at Johns Hopkins University in 1879. He was much beloved by a wide circle of people, and his admiration for the city was expressed in his poem "Ode to the Johns Hopkins University," which includes these lines:

Sit on these Maryland hills, and fix thy reign,
And frame a fairer Athens than of yore.

The library at the Peabody Institute opened in 1866, just a few years before Lanier arrived in Baltimore. Lanier used the library to continue his literary education.

. . .

And many peoples call from shore to shore,
The world has bloomed again at Baltimore![56]

Lanier threw himself into the life of the university with zeal and energy. He was a personal friend of the president, of nearly every member of the faculty, and of the university officers. The result of Lanier's intensive study was the 1879 publication of his book, *The Science of English Verse,* which was described as an admirable "discussion of the relations of music and poetry."[57]

IN THE SUMMER OF 1880, Lanier began his last fight with his old enemy. He wrote to Haynes on November 19:

> For six months past a ghastly fever has been taking possession of me each day at about [noon], and holding my head under the surface of indescribable distress for the next twenty hours, subsiding only enough each morning to let me get on my working-harness, but never intermitting.[58]

Even during his last year, he was cheerful and good-humored. In August, a third son was born, Robert Sampson Lanier, and the father wrote joyful letters to his friends: "I do no labor except works of necessity—such as kissing Mary, who is a more ravishing angel than ever."[59]

Lanier retained all his life a vital Christian faith, though he reacted against the Calvinism of his youth, finding no place for the rigid and severe creed with its narrowness and bigotry. His faith was now as broad as "the liberal marshes of Glynn." One of his intimate friends called Lanier "the most Christlike man I ever knew."[60]

Lanier continued his lectures as long as he was able, but finally in May he traveled with his brother Clifford to the little town of Lynn in the mountains of western North Carolina to try camp life. He died there on September 7, 1881, at the age of thirty-nine. He is buried in Green Mount Cemetery in Baltimore.

Lanier had earlier written to his friend Bayard Taylor: "Pretty much the whole of life has been merely not dying."[61] One of the inspiring things about the Lanier story is what he was able to accomplish, both as a poet and as a musician, in spite of his tragic illness and a short life.

BECAUSE OF LANIER'S SYMPATHY with the ideals of the university and his influence over many of its students, he has a permanent place in the history of Johns Hopkins, which became the repository of his poems and memorabilia. In Gilman Hall there is a room dedicated to poetry. Here the bust of Lanier seems to dominate its surroundings and is greatly admired by visitors and is an inspiration to students.

In 1884 an enlarged and final edition of his poems appeared, prepared by his wife, Mary, who also edited a collection of his letters from 1866–81. These were published in 1889.

In the 1930s, another statue of Lanier was erected in front of Duke Chapel at

The bust of Sidney Lanier in Gilman Hall at Johns Hopkins University, where he lectured for the last two years of his life.

Duke University in Durham, North Carolina. Lanier was placed alongside fellow Southerners Thomas Jefferson and Robert E. Lee, the latter of whom was Lanier's longtime hero.

Today, Sidney Lanier's home state of Georgia honors his legacy with the Sidney Lanier Bridge, the longest bridge in the state, that stretches across the marshes of Glynn County. Three schools and an entire county in Georgia also bear his name.

Lanier is celebrated both throughout the South and across the country. Schools in Alabama, Florida, Virginia, Texas, and Oklahoma are named after him.

The Sidney Lanier High School in Montgomery pays tribute to his time there (1866–67). The original school bearing his name was built in 1910, and in 1929 the name was moved to a

The modern-day Sidney Lanier High School in Montgomery. The Gothic Revival building was called the "million dollar school" when constructed in 1929.

handsome new building in the "Garden District" just south of downtown (the new building consolidated Lanier High School and Montgomery County High School). The high school was predominantly white until the civil rights movement of the 1960s; today, the student body is majority black.

While Sidney Lanier's place in history is set in brick and mortar across the country, his place in literature is also secure as "the leading writer of the New South, the greatest Southern poet of his time since Poe, and a man of heroic and exquisite character."[62]

Notes

1. Edwin Mims, *Sidney Lanier* (Boston: Riverside Press, 1905), 30.
2. Mims, *Sidney Lanier,* 31–32.
3. Ibid., 32.
4. Charles R. Anderson, ed., *Centennial Edition of the Works of Sidney Lanier* (Baltimore: Johns Hopkins Press, 1945), 7:197.
5. Judge Walter B. Jones, "Off the Bench," *Montgomery Advertiser,* January 23, 1933.
6. Anderson, ed. *Centennial Edition,* 7:208.
7. Ibid., 7:209.
8. Ibid., 7:231.
9. Mims, *Sidney Lanier,* 64–66.
10. Ibid., 67.
11. Ibid., 73–74.
12. Ibid., 75.
13. Ibid., 76.
14. Ibid., 80–81.
15. Ibid., 81.
16. Ibid., 86.
17. Anderson, ed. *Centennial Edition,* 7:242.
18. Ibid., 7:272.
19. Ibid., 7:307.

20. Mims, *Sidney Lanier,* 92.
21. Ibid., 97.
22. Ibid., 91–92.
23. Anderson, ed. *Centennial Edition,* 7:338.
24. Ibid., 1:15.
25. Mims, *Sidney Lanier,* 94.
26. Ibid., 106.
27. Anderson, ed. Centennial Edition, 7:354.
28. Ibid., 7:366.
29. Ibid., 8:265.
30. Mims, *Sidney Lanier,* 97.
31. Ibid., 101–103.
32. Ibid., 121.
33. Ibid., 121–122.
34. Ibid., 123.
35. Ibid., 124–125.
36. Ibid., 130.
37. Ibid., 152.
38. Ibid., 308.
39. Ibid., 131–132.
40. Ibid., 133.
41. Ibid., 134.
42. Ibid., 144–147.
43. Ibid., 148.
44. Anderson, ed. *Centennial Edition,* 10:376–377.
45. Mims, *Sidney Lanier,* 190.
46. Edmund Fuller and Jo B. Kinnick, *Adventures in American Literature* (New York: Harcourt, Brace, and World, 1963), 743.
47. Mims, *Sidney Lanier,* 196.
48. Fuller and Kinnick, *American Literature,* 744–745.
49. Jack Debellis, *Sidney Lanier: Poet of the Marshes.* Athens, Georgia: Georgia Center for Continuing Education, 1983. Videocassette (VHS), 28 min.
50. Mims, *Sidney Lanier,* 369.
51. Ibid., 318–319.
52. Fuller and Kinnick, *American Literature,* 746–749.
53. Mims, *Sidney Lanier,* 199.
54. Ibid., 200.

55. Ibid., 204.
56. Ibid., 230.
57. Ibid., 359.
58. Ibid., 321.
59. Ibid., 324.
60. Ibid., 318.
61. Ibid., 67.
62. *Encyclopædia Britannica*, 11th ed., s.v. "Lanier, Sidney."

Sources of Illustrations

Page 2: Historic Macon Foundation
Page 4: University System of Georgia Archives
Page 7: From "Letters of Sidney Lanier" at the Internet Archive (archive. org)
Page 8: State Library and Archives of Florida
Pages 12, 14, 15: Courtesy of Mary Ann Neeley
Page 16: Alabama Department of Archives and History.
Page 20: Helen Blackshear files
Page 24, 30: Library of Congress
Page 39: Golden Isles Georgia
Page 41: Matthew Petroff
Page 40: Library of Congress
Page 43: Johns Hopkins University
Page 44: Chris Pruitt

Index

CPSIA information can be obtained
at www.ICGtesting.com
Printed in the USA
JSHW021211300720
6985JS00005B/89